THE NEW SAMSUNG S24 ULTRA USER GUIDE FOR ALL CATEGORIES

A guide that captures all the new features and how to perfectly utilize them

Joy Matthew

Table of Contents

INTRODUCTION

The Samsung Galaxy S24 UItra features a quad-camera system with AI support. Its cameras are equipped with 12MP, 50MP, and 10MP sensors, and it can record 8K videos. In addition, it has a 5X telephoto lens and optical image stabilization.

The Samsung Galaxy S24 UItra is powered by a Qualcomm Snapdragon 8 Gen 3 processor. It has 4 GB of RAM and 64 GB of storage.

The Samsung Galaxy S24 UItra will be using the Snapdragon 3 chipset, which will affect its performance.

The Ultra version of the Samsung Galaxy S24 will be getting the latest Exynos chipset. Its high-speed processing capabilities make it an ideal device for users. The regular Galaxy S24 and S24 Plus will also receive an update with the new Exynos chipset.

The Samsung Galaxy S24 UItra has 8GB of RAM and 128GB of storage. It's a smartphone that's powered by

Android. It comes with various features such as Bluetooth, GPS, and USB Type-C.

This device is powered by a 5100mAh battery and has a 6.8-inch display. It comes with a quad camera system that's capable of shooting at a resolution of 1440 x 3200 pixels.

It has two SIM card slots, and a 32MP camera is included on the front. The Samsung Galaxy S24UItra utilizes a variety of sensors, such as proximity, compass, display fingerprint, and barometer.

The 24MP camera found on the Samsung Galaxy 24 UItra is quite impressive. It's believed that this device's camera resolution is better than that of the Galaxy S23, which has 12MP. It has also reportedly a photo remaster feature, which allows users to remove shadows from their photos.

The Galaxy S24 UItra offers different options for users, such as erasing, remastering, and portrait. Its ND filter, which is a neutral density filter, can help users change the brightness and colors of their photos.

The AI capabilities of the S24 Ultra, which is an upgraded version of the Galaxy S24, will allow users to take high-quality videos and capture specific zoomed-in areas.

Users no longer need to manually adjust the settings on their devices due to the capabilities of the AI system and the ability to capture moving objects. With the Samsung Galaxy S24UITRA, users can enjoy a better and smoother experience when shooting videos.

Key features

Camera xCloud

Take great close-up photos of your subject and enjoy high-quality gaming using your mobile device. You can also view the scenes of each camera through the xCloud service.

Samsung DeX

With the DeX wireless connection, you can multitask on a big screen. You can refer to Samsung for more information.

S Pen

You can use the S Pen to control the device's screen. You can experience a seamless smartphone experience by connecting it to a computer. You can refer to Microsoft for more information.

Link to Windows

Your smartphone should be connected to a computer so that you can experience a seamless experience. You can refer to Microsoft through the link provided.

CHAPTER ONE

Device layout and functions

Hard keys

The main function of the hard keys is to turn on and lock the device. You can start a dialogue with Bixby by holding and pressing it. You can also press and hold on the volume down or double-press the right side to launch the app and feature you want to use. You can also take a screenshot by simultaneously pressing both of these keys.

Setting the Side key

To launch a feature or app, double-press the Side key twice or hold it while pressing it.

To navigate to the Advanced features section, go to the Settings app, choose the option you want, and then click on the Side key.

Soft buttons

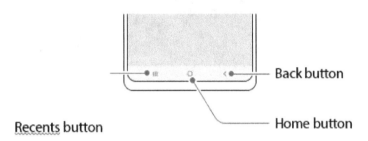

The soft buttons will be at the bottom of the device's screen when you turn on the device. You can navigate through the navigation bar for more information.

Wireless power sharing

Even though you have your device's battery charged, you can still use it to power another device. The issue with this feature is that it may not work properly if there are certain accessories or covers that you're using.

Smartphone   Galaxy Watch   Galaxy Buds

Go to the notification panel and swipe downwards. Then tap "Wireless power sharing" to activate it.

When you're done charging, disconnect the device from yours to prevent it from affecting nearby gadgets. You should also avoid using headphones while using wireless power.

The wireless charging location of your device may vary depending on the model. To ensure proper connection, adjust the devices' respective settings.

Some of the features that are included in the wireless power sharing feature may not work while you're using it.

Only certain models support wireless power sharing and may be used to charge other devices. You can check for these through the Samsung site.

Never use or move both devices while charging to ensure proper usage. Also, the power used to power the other device may be lower than that provided by your device.

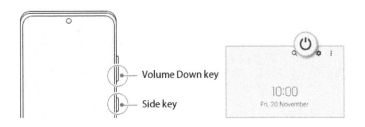

Charging the other device while using wireless power may result in slower charging speed or the device not charging properly.

The charging efficiency and speed of a particular device may vary depending on its environment and condition.

Setting the limit for power sharing

You can configure your device to stop sharing power when the battery level drops below a certain point.

Go to the Settings app and select "Battery" and "Device Care." Then choose "Limit Wireless Power Sharing."

The gadget should be turned on and off.

In case you happen to be in a restricted area, such as hospitals or airplanes, follow the posted warnings and instructions to avoid using wireless devices.

Turn on the device

Hold the power key for a few seconds and turn the device on. Then turn off the device.

Turning the device off

Press and hold the Volume Down and Side keys at the same time to deactivate the device. You can also swipe downwards and tap on the notification panel to open it.2 Tap Power off.

You can set your device to automatically turn off using the Side key press and hold it. You can access the Advanced features through the Settings app and then choose Power off.

Forcing restart

After your device has stopped working and is unresponsive, press the volume down and side keys simultaneously for about 7 seconds to restart.

Emergency mode

To conserve battery life, turn off your device in emergency mode. This will allow you to use certain functions and apps while keeping some of them restricted. Among these are making an emergency call and sending your location to other people.

To activate emergency mode, hold both the volume down and side keys at the same time. Then, go to the notification panel and swipe downwards.

Tap the option "Turn off Emergency Mode" to deactivate it.

The battery life displayed on the device shows the amount of time that remains before the device's battery will run out.

CHAPTER TWO

Initial setup

Follow the instructions provided on the screen to set up your device after it has been turned on or after it has been reset.

Setting up the device and performing other tasks may be difficult if you're not connected to a Wi-Fi network.

Samsung account

Through your Samsung account, you can access a wide range of services offered by mobile phones, TV displays, and the official Samsung site.

You can also check the list of services that are available to you through your Samsung account by visiting account.samsung.com.

You can also check the list of available services for your Samsung account by visiting account.samsung.COM. To access the settings app, go to the settings.

Go to the settings app and select Account and Backup. You can also manage your various accounts and add a new Samsung account.

If you're already a Samsung user, you can sign in to your account. On the other hand, if you're a Google user, you can access your account by pressing Continue. If you're not a Samsung user, you can create a new account. You can also look for your ID and reset your password.

Finding your ID and resetting your password

On the sign-in page, tap the option "Find ID" or "Reset password." You can then find your ID and reset your password by entering the required information.

You can sign out of Samsung's account by going to the sign-in screen and selecting "Find ID" and "Reset password."

Your contacts, calendar events, and other information will be deleted from your device once you have signed out of your Samsung account.

Go to the Settings app and select Account and backup.
Then, go to Manage your accounts.

Go to the Samsung account sign-in page and select My
profile. Then, enter your password and sign out.

You can also transfer data from your old device to your
new one.

Smart Switch

The Smart Switch app allows you to transfer data from an
old device to a new one. You can do this by launching the
Settings app and selecting Account and backup.

Unfortunately, this feature may not work on some
computers and devices.

The Smart Switch app and its features are only limited to
certain types of activities. You should only use it if you
have the right to do so and are authorized to do so.

Transferring data using a USB cable

The easiest way to transfer data from your old gadget to your new one is through a USB cable.

The previous device must be connected using your gadget's USB cable. Sometimes, a USB connector is required for the older model.

After the app selection screen appears, tap on the "Get data" button. In the previous device, choose "Allow." If you don't have the app, you can download it from the Play Store or Galaxy Store. You'll then see a list of the data that you can transfer as your device recognizes the previous one.

Disconnecting the USB cable while you're transferring files may cause your device to malfunction.

Data transfer can use up your device's battery. Before you start using it, make sure that it's charged. Low battery power can prevent data from being sent.

Transferring data wirelessly

Wi-Fi Direct is the preferred method of transferring data from your old device to a newer one. To use this feature, launch the Smart Switch app on the previous device. If you don't have it, you can download it from either the Play Store or the Galaxy Store. You can then go to the Settings app and select Backup and Account.

Place the two devices close to each other. In the previous device, choose "Send data wirelessly." On your gadget, choose "Transfer." You can then choose to transfer backup data from a computer.

Transferring backup data from a computer

You can use the computer version of the Smart Switch app to transfer data between the two devices. You must download it from the website of Samsung. You can also restore your old device's data and import it to your gadget.

To download the app, go to the website of Samsung at www.samsung.com. Then, launch Smart Switch on the computer.

If the previous device is not made by Samsung, you can still use a program that the manufacturer provides to back up your data to a computer. Doing so will allow you to perform the fifth step.

Go to the computer and connect your old device to it using the USB cable. Follow the on-screen prompts to restore and transfer data from your device. Then, disconnect the old device from the computer.

You can learn how to control the touchscreen by holding it for a couple of seconds. Double-tapping on the device and holding it down for a couple of seconds will allow you to drag and double-tap it to the desired position. You can also use various gestures such as swiping, pinching, and squeezing upward or downwards to spread two fingers across the left or right side of the screen.

Keep away from touching other electrical devices to prevent the touchscreen from malfunctioning. The touchscreen may be affected by electrostatic discharge.

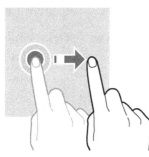

Do not tap the touchscreen using sharp objects or excessively pressure it with your fingertips to prevent it from getting damaged.

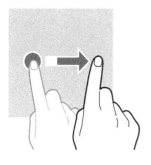

For extended periods of time, it's recommended to avoid using the touchscreen with fixed graphics. Doing so could cause ghosting or afterimages.

The device may not recognize certain touch inputs near the edges of the display.

Navigation bar (soft buttons)

The navigation bar located at the bottom of your device's screen will show you the soft buttons, which are usually set to the Home, Recents, and Back buttons. The functions of these buttons can vary depending on the current app or environment that you're using.

The Recents button lets you open the list of apps. The Home button returns to the home screen. On the other hand, the Back button returns to the previous screen while the Google Assistant app launches. To hide the navigation bar, go to the Applications section and choose View files.

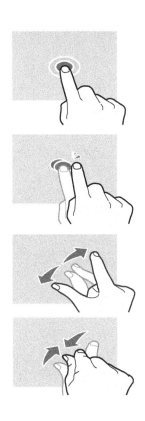

Go to the Settings app and scroll to the navigation bar. Then, under the navigation type, swipe your finger across the right side to reveal the hidden navigation bar. You'll then be able to see the gesture hints and select the option that you want.

To remove the navigation bar from the bottom and sides of the screen, swipe from the left to the right side.

Button		Function
III	Recents	• Tap to open the list of recent apps.
O	Home	• Tap to return to the Home screen. • Tap and hold to launch the **Google Assistant** app.
<	Back	• Tap to return to the previous screen.

Gesture hints can be deactivated if you wish to hide them at the bottom of the screen.

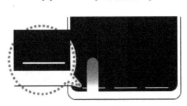

Swipe from bottom   Swipe from sides and bottom

Home screen and Apps screen

The home screen serves as the primary area where you can access the device's various features. It displays various shortcuts and tools, as well as apps and widgets.

The Apps screen is where you can find all the recently installed apps and their icons. You can switch between the home and apps screens by swiping upwards.

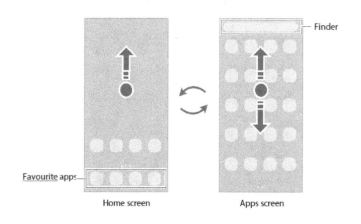

Home screen   Apps screen

To return to the home screen, swipe upward or downwards on the apps screen. You can also tap either the Back or Home buttons.

Adding the apps button to the home screen will let you open the apps screen. To activate this feature, tap on the empty area in the home screen and then tap on the Show Apps button. The app will be added to the bottom of the home screen.

Apps button

Editing the Home screen

To access the home screen's editing options, tap on the empty area and hold it. You can customize the wallpaper, add and remove widgets, and rearrange the various home screen panels.

To add panels, swipe to the left and then tap on the "Add panels" button.

To move or add panels, tap and hold the preview and drag it to wherever you want it to be. You can also change the settings for the home screen and its locked screen.

The device's theme can be changed. The visual elements of the interface, such as the wallpapers, icons, and colors, will change according to the chosen theme.

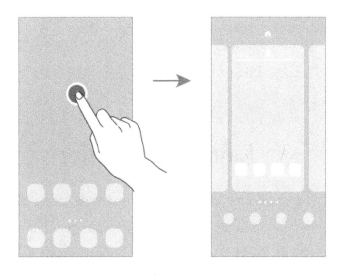

Small apps that serve specific functions are known as "widgets." They can provide you with additional information and quick access to the home screen. To add a widget, select it from the list and then tap on "Add."

You can configure the settings of the home screen and view all applications in one place.

You can set your device to show all the installed apps on the home screen without using an app screen. To do so, tap on the home screen and hold the empty area. You can then go to the settings app and select the layout of the home screen that you want.

To access all of your installed apps, swipe left on the home screen.

Launching Finder

You can now access your installed apps using the left swipe on the home screen, and you can also launch the Finder to quickly find all of the content on your device.

On the Apps screen, go to the search bar and tap on the option that says "Search." Alternatively, you can open the notification section and swipe downwards.

Drag the item to wherever you want it to be and then tap and hold it. You can also move it to another part of the screen by dragging it to the side.

To add a shortcut for an app to the home screen go to the Apps screen and hold an item there. You can then tap on the Add to Home button. You can also choose which shortcuts to move to on the home screen depending on which apps are frequently used.

Creating folders

Folders can be created to organize similar apps so you can easily access and launch them. Drag one app over another in the home screen or the apps screen to create a new folder containing the ones that you've selected.

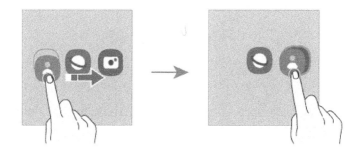

Go to the folder where you want to add an app and click on Done. You can also drag one to the folder and add it manually.

In this case, you would like to move apps from one folder to another.

Drag and hold an app in order to move it to a different location. Similarly, you can Delet a folder.

To remove a folder, go to the folder and hold it. Then, click on the Delete button to remove only the folder. The apps will be moved to the Apps screen as the folders will be deleted.

Hold the folder and click the Delete button. The only thing that will be deleted is the folder. All of the apps in it will be relocated to your apps screen.

Edge panel

The Edge panels allow you to easily access your favorite features and apps. Drag the panel handle to the center of the screen.

If the Edge panel's handle is not visible, go to the Settings app and tap on the Display option. You can then activate it by pressing the switch.

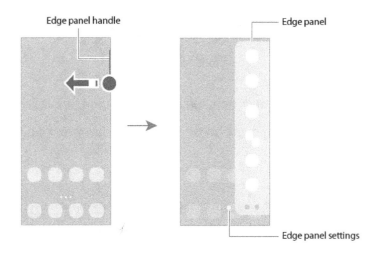

Edge panel handle

Edge panel

Edge panel settings

Lock screen

The Side key can be used to turn off the device and lock it. Similarly, the screen will automatically turn off whenever the device is not being used.

You can unlock the screen by swiping in any direction whenever the screen turns on.

Turn on the device by pressing the Side key. Double-tapping the screen will also turn it on.

Changing the screen lock method

Launch the Settings app and navigate to the Lock screen option. You can then choose the method that you want to use.

You can protect your information by setting up a pattern, password, PIN, or biometric data to prevent unauthorized access to your device. After you have enabled the screen lock option, your device will need an unlock code to use.

If you're having issues with the unlock code repeatedly, you can enable factory data reset on your device. This method will prevent the device from accessing the latest version of its software. You can also use the pre-defined screen lock method to access the lock screen.

Indicator icons

Icon	Meaning
⊘	No signal
.ıll	Signal strength
ᴿᵢll	Roaming (outside of normal service area)
G	GPRS network connected
E	EDGE network connected
3G	UMTS network connected
H	HSDPA network connected
H+	HSPA+ network connected

Icon	Meaning
4G / LTE	LTE network connected
5G	5G network connected
5G	LTE network connected in LTE network that includes the 5G network
🛜	Wi-Fi connected
⁑	Bluetooth feature activated
○	Location services being used
⁑	Bluetooth feature activated
○	Location services being used
📞	Call in progress
⤳	Missed call
▬	New text or multimedia message
⏰	Alarm activated
◀ / ◀	Mute mode / Vibration mode
✈	Flight mode activated
⚠	Error occurred or caution required
/	Battery charging / Battery power level

The status bar on your device displays various icons. The most frequently used ones are shown in the table below.

The icons are related to the type of connectivity that the device has with its 5G network. They show the various services that are activated when using the 5G network, such as calls, texts, and multimedia messages. Some of these include the alarm and vibration modes.

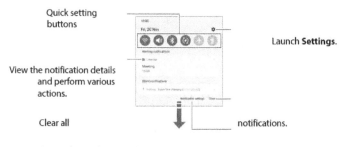

Quick setting buttons

Launch **Settings**.

View the notification details and perform various actions.

Clear all

notifications.

Access the notification settings.

Some applications may not feature a status bar at the top of the screen. To view it, drag it down from the top portion of the screen.

Some of the indicator icons will only appear after you open the notification section.

The appearance of some of the indicator icons may vary depending on the model or service provider.

Notification panel

The status bar displays the various indicator icons that are associated with the new notifications that you receive. To see the details of these icons, go to the notification section and open it.

Drag the status bar down to open the notification section. Release it and then swipe upward to close the panel.

The notification panel has various features that you can utilize. You can launch the settings, view the details of the notifications, perform various actions, and clear all of them. You can also access the settings by using quick setting.

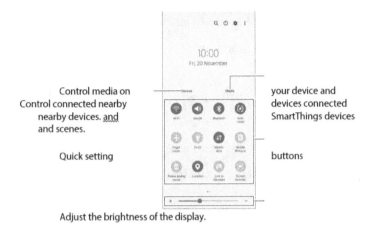

Control media on
Control connected nearby
nearby devices. and
and scenes.

your device and
devices connected
SmartThings devices

Quick setting

buttons

Adjust the brightness of the display.

To activate certain features, tap on the quick setting button. Scroll down to the notification section and tap on the additional buttons.

Control media on your device

You can control different media players and devices through their respective networks. You can also access the settings for connected gadgets and scenes.

Tap the text under each of the buttons to change the feature preferences. Tapping and holding a button will take you to the detailed settings page.

To change the arrangement of the buttons, tap on the Edit button and hold it. Release it and drag it to another part of the screen.

Controlling media playback

The media feature allows users to easily control the playback of various types of media files on their device.

Go to the notification section, swipe downwards, and then open the media feature. Release the dock and tap on the icons to control the playback.

To continue the playback of your device on another one, tap and select it from the list of options. You can also control the nearby devices.

You can easily control the various gadgets connected to your device and those used by SmartThings using the notification panel.

Go to the notification section and swipe downwards. You can see the list of connected gadgets and scenes and choose which one you want to control. You can also launch a scene or select a nearby gadget to control.

Screen capture

You can easily capture a screenshot of the current screen while using the device. You can also crop, draw on, or share it.

How to capture a screenshot

You can utilize the following methods to take screenshots. They can be conveniently viewed in the Gallery.

One method is by pressing both the Volume Down and Side keys at the same time. Another method is by swiping across the right or left side of the screen.

Unfortunately, it is not always possible to take screenshots while using certain features and apps.

If you are not able to capture a screenshot using the swiping method, you can try to access the settings app and select Advanced features. Then, tap the Palm swipe to activate the feature.

After you have captured a screenshot, go to the toolbar located at the bottom of the screen and choose the options that you want.

The goal of this feature is to capture the current state and the hidden content of an article or a page, which can be accessed by clicking on it.

You can crop or write a portion of the screenshot or draw on it. It can be conveniently viewed in the Gallery.

Navigate to the Apps screen and click on the "Search" button at the top. Then, tap "Screenshots" to view the list of tags and search for the ones that you want.

Compose and distribute the screenshot.

When the options are not displayed on the screen, go to the Settings app and open the Advanced features section. Then, tap the "Screenshot toolbar switch" to activate the feature.

Screen record

You can record a ⊕screen while you're using your device. To activate this feature, go to the notification panel and swipe downwards. You can then select the sound setting and start recording by pressing the "Start recording" button. You can also take a screenshot by tapping on the video overlay of yourself.

Go to the Settings app and select the Advanced features. Then, go to the ✎Screenshots and Screen Recorder section.

When you type a text message, a keyboard appears automatically. There are also various keyboard functions that you can use to input various words. For example, you can replace the first letter with an uppercase letter, change the capitalization for all caps, and enter spaces.

Some languages do not support text entry. To use this feature, you need to change the input language.

Changing the input language is required in order to use this feature.

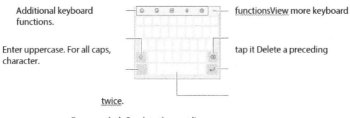

Additional keyboard functions.

functionsView more keyboard

Enter uppercase. For all caps, character.

tap it Delete a preceding

twice.

Enter symbols.Break to the next line.

In the Languages and Types section, go to the Manage input languages option and select the ones that you want to use. You can also switch between them by swiping to the right or left on the space key.

Changing the keyboard

To change the keyboard, go to the navigation bar and tap on it.

Go to the Languages and Types section and select the language that you want to use. Then, choose the keyboard type that you want to use.

If the navigation bar does not show the keyboard button, go to the Settings app and open the General management section. Then, select the Keyboard option and tap on the button to activate it.

A standard 3 x 4 keyboard has up to four characters. To type a character, you can tap the corresponding key multiple times until it appears.

Additional keyboard functions are available, such as the ability to type emojis.

Emoji stickers can also be used to add a personal touch to your message. You can learn more about using emojis in chats by referring to your own stickers.

To attach animated GIF files, you can use voice to enter text. You can also change the keyboard settings and use handwriting mode to improve its performance. In addition, you can search for content, enter it, and register your Samsung Pass account.

You can add an item from the clipboard and open the text editing panel. You can also change the keyboard mode, keyboard size, and more. Some features may not work on certain models or service providers. To copy and paste text, hold over it and tap on it. You can then choose the text that you want to use by either dragging or selecting it.

To copy or cut the selected text, go to the Clipboard app and tap on the Paste button. You can also select the text that you want to paste by holding the desired location and pressing the button. You can download or install apps that are specific for your Samsung Galaxy device.

To start using the Galaxy Store app, browse through the categories or look for a keyword. This app may not work on certain models or service providers. To change the settings for automatic updates, go to the Auto update option and select an option. You can also download or purchase apps from the Play Store.

Go to the category or keyword search bar and browse through the various categories. You can then change the auto update option by pressing the "Settings" button and selecting "Auto-update apps." Turning off or managing the apps You can select which ones to remove and which ones to disable.

In order to use this feature, some apps may not support it. To enable it, go to the Settings app and select the option that you want to enable. Then select an app from the list and enable its permissions.

Some apps may need to have permission to access and use your device's data.

Launch the Settings app and navigate to the apps section. On the left-hand screen, choose the category that you want to view and tap on the permissions. You can then view and change the permissions of the app.

To see and change the permissions for each app, go to the Settings app, select the category that you want to view, and then click on the "app manager" button.

The basic functions of apps may not work if you do not allow them to have permissions.

CHAPTER THREE

Phone

Answer or make a video or voice call.

2 Enter a phone number.
3 Tap to make a voice call, or tap to make a video call.

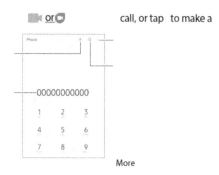

Unnecessary noises may occur during calls if the area around the microphone is covered. To prevent this, remove any accessories that are around the microphone, such as stickers or a screen protector.

Making calls

To make calls from your contacts list or call logs, go to the Phone app and tap on the Keypad.

To make a call, go to the Phone app and select Contacts or Recents. Then, swipe to the right on the contact or the phone number that you want to call.

Go to the Settings app and choose the category that you wish to view, then click on the "other call settings" button. You can then activate this feature by pressing the "text switch" or "call" button.

Using speed dial

You can set a speed dial number by going to the Phone app, selecting the option, and then adding a contact number.

Dialing a speed dial number using the keypad requires holding the first and last digits of the number. For numbers 10 and up, you can tap the first digit and hold the last one.

For instance, if you want to set 123 as a speed dialing number, you can first tap the number one, two, and three.

Setting a speed dial number for international calls will allow you to make calls to other countries.

To initiate an international call, go to your Phone app and tap the Keypad. You can then enter the country code, the area code, and the phone number. You can then choose to receive or reject calls. Answering calls while dragging outside the large circle or rejecting them.

When you reject an incoming call, you can send a message by dragging the Send message bar up and down.

Go to the Phone app and choose the option to create a variety of rejection messages. Drag the message bar up and down and then enter the text message.

Blocking phone numbers

You can block incoming calls from numbers in your block list that you have added. To block these calls, go to the Settings app and select the option "Block numbers".

Go to Contacts or Recents, select the phone numbers or contacts that you want to add, and then select Done. You can also manually enter the numbers by pressing the Add Phone Number option, entering the number, and then pressing OK.

You can also block calls from numbers that do not have the caller ID of the person who is calling. To activate this feature, go to the Contacts or Recents section and select the option to block private or unknown numbers.

Options during calls

The second call can be initiated by pressing the "add call." The first one will be put on hold, and the second will be resumed if you end the session.

You may press the "hold" button to initiate a call. You may also use a Bluetooth headset if you are connected to a device.

Keep your device away from your ears while using the speakerphone. You can either deactivate or activate the speakerphone.

Turn off the microphone to mute the other party's ability to hear you.

The other party will no longer hear you. Turning off the microphone mutes the other party from hearing you. You can also close or open the keypad. Turning off the camera during a video call blocks the other party from seeing you. Switching between the rear and front cameras allows you to make the call disappear.

Some of the features may not work on certain models or service providers. You can create new contacts or manage existing ones on your device. To start the process, go to the app and select the "Create New Contact" button. You can also select a storage location and enter the contact information.

You can easily add contacts from other devices by launching the Contacts app and selecting Import or Export contacts. Follow the instructions provided on the screen to import contacts or sync them with your web accounts.

You can sync your contacts from your device to your web accounts, which include your Samsung account.

Tap the Settings app and select the backup and account options. Then, select the sync option to use the account you want to sync with.

To activate the sync option, tap the Contacts switch. You can also start a search for your contacts by going to the top of the list and entering the search criteria. After selecting the contact, you can perform various actions such as making a voice call or composing a message.

To create an email, go to the Contacts app and select the option "Delete contacts." You can then select the ones that you want to remove from the list. You can also delete multiple contacts by going to the top of the list and selecting "Select contacts." Sharing contacts With Others You can allow others to share the contact information with them.

To share contacts, go to the Contacts app and select the option "Share contacts." You can then choose the sharing method that you want. You can also create groups, which can be composed of friends or family members. Follow the steps provided on the screen to complete the process.

Merging duplicate contacts

Merge duplicate contacts into one so that your contacts list becomes more streamlined.

Voice messages can be recorded by pressing and holding the record button, saying the message, and releasing your finger. The icon for recording appears only while the input field is empty.

Go to the Contacts app and select the option "Manage contacts." Then, tap on the "Merge contacts" button. You can also send and receive messages 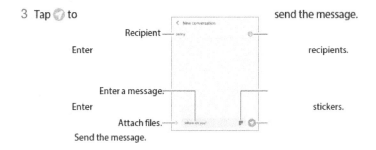using the app. However, you might incur additional charges when you're on the go.

3 Tap to   send the message.
                          Recipient —— Jelly
      Enter   recipients.

              Enter a message.
      Enter   stickers.
          Attach files.——> Where are you?
      Send the message.

Viewing messages

Launch the Messages app and select the option "Conversations." On the list, choose a phone number or contact and then tap on the input field to reply to the message. To change the font size, tap on the screen or spread two fingers apart. You can also sort your messages by category to make them easier to manage.

Go to the Settings app and select the category option for conversations. If the option does not appear, follow the steps provided on the screen to activate it.

Deleting messages

Hold the message and select the option to remove it. Then, tap on the option to change the settings.

To change the settings or block unwanted messages, go to the settings section of the Messages app.

Internet

You can easily access the Internet's various resources by browsing for information and leaving a bookmark for your favorite sites.

Go to the Internet app and enter your web address. You can then view the toolbars and switch between the tabs by dragging your finger down on the screen.

Using secret mode

Setting up a password for secret mode will prevent others from accessing your saved pages, search history, bookmarks, and browsing history.

Go to the secret mode settings and select the "lock down" option.

To activate the secret mode, go to the Lock mode switch, select Start, and then set the password for it.

The secret mode doesn't allow you to use certain features, such as the ability to capture screen shots.

CHAPTER FOUR

Camera

Screen capture is not enabled in secret mode. You can still take photos and record videos through various settings and modes. Camera etiquette: Do not take pictures or videos of other individuals without their permission, and ensure that you do not take such actions while filming in areas that are legally restricted.

You should refrain from taking photos or videos in places that could violate the privacy of others. You can launch the Camera app to take photos.

The app can be launched by pressing the Side key multiple times or dragging it to the left while in the locked screen.

Some of the camera app's features are unavailable when you launch it from the locked screen or while the screen is turned off.

Drag the adjustment bar over or below the circular frame to change the brightness of your pictures.

To take a shot, 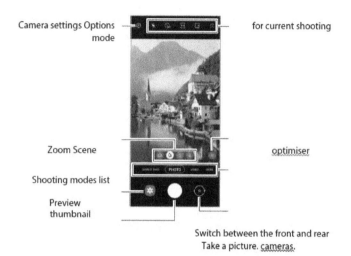 tap on the button next to the camera app.

Drag the list of shooting options to the right or left and choose the mode that you want to use.

Camera settings Options mode — for current shooting

Zoom Scene — optimiser

Shooting modes list

Preview thumbnail

Switch between the front and rear
Take a picture. cameras.

The preview screen may change based on the mode used and the kind of camera being used.

High-speed cameras with a large zoom range or a distorted image may not focus properly on the subject close to you. Instead, take photos at a reasonable distance.

If your photos are blurry, try cleaning the lens.

61

Make sure that the lens of your device is not contaminated or damaged. Issues such as this may prevent the device from performing properly in high-quality settings.

The camera of your device has a wide lens. Minor distortion can occur in photos and videos with wide-angle lenses, though it does not necessarily mean that the device has issues with performance. To fix this issue, go to the preview screen and tap on the option that says "Advanced," "Format," and "Ultra Wide Shape Correction."

The maximum amount of video that you can take with your device varies depending on the resolution.

Using zoom features

To use the zoom feature, ∞ / ∞ / ◊ / ◊ select or drag the lens to either the left or right side of the screen. You can also use the two-finger technique to zoom in and out. If the zoom level exceeds a certain value, a map will appear that indicates where you are focusing.

The Ultra wide camera can take photos and videos of subjects that are beyond the usual scope, such as landscapes.

The wide-angle camera can take photos and videos of ordinary objects. On the other hand, the 3x zoom lens allows you to magnify the subject in photos.

The Galaxy S24 Ultra 5G has a 10x zoom lens that allows users to take photos and record videos with enhanced subject sizes.

The rear camera has the exclusive zoom capabilities.

Only the rear camera has these capabilities. You can lock the focus and aperture on photos with this feature.

This feature can also lock the exposure and focus on a specific area to prevent the device from automatically adjusting according to changes in the light sources or subjects in the photo.

Hold the area you want to focus on and the AF/AE frame will show up. You can then lock the exposure and focus settings.

This feature may not work on certain shooting modes.

Using the camera button

You may not use this feature on photos taken in certain shooting modes. To take a video, tap on the camera button and hold it. You can also take burst shots by swiping the camera button from the edge of the screen.

Adding a camera button to your device can make it easier to take photos, as it can be moved anywhere on the screen. To activate it, tap the "Floating Shutter Button" switch on the preview screen.

Options for current shooting mode

The preview screen provides various options for shooting mode. You can ⚡ deactivate or activate the flash. You can also set the delay before the camera takes a shot, and choose the aspect 🕐 ratio of the ▭ pictures.

Motion photo may be activated or deactivated. With the activation of this feature, a video clip will take a few seconds before you tap the camera button.

The motion photo feature may be deactivated or activated. With the feature enabled, a video clip will be taken from a few seconds prior to the tap of the camera button.

Deactivate or deactivate the stabilization feature for videos. Choose a video's resolution, frame rate, aspect ratio, and more. You can apply a beauty effect or filter effect.

A metering method is important when it comes to calculating light values. The method that you select will determine how the light is used in the shot. Center-weighted is used to determine the exposure of the shot, while Spot uses the light in the center portion of the shot to determine the exposure, and Matrix averages the whole scene.

In auto ⊞ focus mode, you can change the focus area on your photos. For instance, you can use multi-focused mode to focus on different areas within the frame. Centre focuses on the center.

You can choose a resolution that's ideal for videos, and set the light distribution in your photos. You can also hide or display a graph to analyze the distribution of light in the footage. In FOOD mode, you can focus on a subject within the frame's circular portion and blur the image externally.

In DIRECTOR'S VIEW mode, you can select the screen layout. When taking single photos, you can customize the options to suit your needs. The settings may vary for different cameras and shooting modes.

Photo mode

The camera automatically adjusts its settings depending on the environment to take photos conveniently.

To take a photo, tap the PHOTO button and select the shooting mode that you want to use.

You can take high-quality pictures with this method.

High-quality photos can be taken with this method. You can crop them to get a better resolution or save them as a high-quality file.

The options for taking photos are shown in the menu. Depending on the model, the resolution may vary. You can also optimize the photos for the best possible effect.

Optimiser

When the camera recognizes the subject, the settings will change and the effect and color will be applied.

Tap on the preview screen if the feature is not enabled, and then tap the Scene Optimizer switch to activate it.

Shot suggestions

The camera can recommend the appropriate composition based on your subject's angle and position.

To activate Shot suggestions, tap on the preview screen and follow the steps given below. You'll then see a guide that will show the appropriate composition for your subject.

The suggested composition appears in the preview screen after the camera has recognized the subject.

To change the guide's composition, go to the device and reposition it. Once you get the ideal shot, it will change to yellow. Selfies are also an option.

Taking selfies

Go to the preview screen and swipe upward or downwards. Alternatively, tap on the front camera for selfies.

You can ⊗take a wide-angle self-portrait using the front camera or shoot a clear close-up shot of your subject using the Galaxy S21 Ultra.

When the ⊙ option appears, ✿ tap to take a ◯ photo. If the feature is not enabled, tap to ⊙ activate it. You can apply various beauty effects and filters to your photos.

Applying filter and beauty effects

Before taking a picture, select a filter effect that you want to apply to your face. You can also modify facial features such as the shape of your face or your skin tone.

Go to the preview screen ✿ and tap on the effect that you want to apply.

Take ⊙ a picture after ⊗ choosing your preferred effects.

You can use the My filters feature to create your own filter by choosing an image with a certain color tone.

Video mode

The camera automatically adjusts the settings depending on the scene to make capturing videos easier.

Tap the video option in the list and then tap "record a video."

To switch between the two cameras while taking a video, go to the preview screen and swipe upward or downwards.

You can use this to take a picture while recording video.

To play the recording of the sound at a specific pitch while shooting videos at a higher volume, point the camera toward the desired direction and change the zoom.

To stop recording, go to the preview screen and swipe upward or downwards.

For prolonged use of the video zoom feature, your device may experience issues with video quality, which could prevent it from overheating.

If you're planning on using the optical zoom feature in low-light conditions, you might have to rethink your choice. Instead, try recording videos with a resolution of up to 8K.

After you've finished recording a video, go back to the Gallery app and play it. Tap on the frame that you want to use, and it will be converted into a high-quality image.

To stabilize your videos, use the Super Steady feature.

Go to the list of shooting modes and tap on the video option. Then tap on the options to activate it and shoot a video.

Director's view mode

You can use this mode to record videos with different angles of view by changing the cameras. It allows both the person filming and the subject to be captured at the same time.

To start recording, go to the list of shooting modes and tap on the video option. Then choose the screen that you want to use and the camera thumbnail that you want to record.

As you take a video, the camera's thumbnail can be changed. If it's hidden, tap to show it.

To stop recording, tap on the button next to the video option.

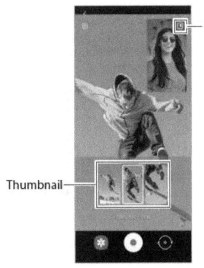

Thumbnail

Change the screen.

Single take mode

You can take multiple photos and videos in a single shot using this mode.

The device will automatically choose the best shot and produce videos with repetitive sections.

Go to the list of shooting modes and tap on the single take option. Then choose the scene that you want to capture.

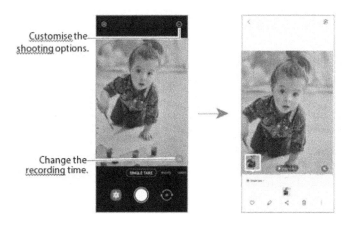

Customise the shooting options.

Change the recording time.

AR Doodle mode

You can record videos with drawings or virtual handwriting on your face or other surfaces. To find more information about this feature, refer to "AR Doodle."

Pro mode / Pro video mode

You can take photos and videos while adjusting the ISO and exposure values manually.

To find the different shooting modes, tap on the "More" button next to the "Pro" or "Video" option. You can then customize the settings and take a video or take a photo.

Select the type of audio that you want to record at a certain level. You can connect a Bluetooth or USB microphone to your device through the Pro video mode.

ISO values are used to control the sensitivity of the camera. Low values are for brightly lit objects, while high ISO values can cause noise in videos and photos.

The shutter speed can be adjusted to get the most out of your photos and videos. For example, a slow shutter speed helps create a brighter image while allowing you to capture more light at night. On the other hand, a fast shutter speed is ideal for capturing subjects moving fast.

Change the exposure value to determine how much light the sensor can receive. For low light conditions, use a higher setting.

You can change the focus mode by dragging the adjustment bar or manually adjusting it. You can then switch to an auto focus mode by pressing the "Manual" button.

Change the tone of the color.

Zoom speed can be adjusted in the Pro video mode.

If you manually set the shutter speed, you won't be able to set the ISO or exposure values. The exposure will be adjusted based on the speed.

To record high-quality videos, tap on the "Pro" button and select the option to use the 8K resolution.

After you've finished recording a video, open the Gallery app and play it. Tap on the frame that you want to use, and it will be converted into a high-quality image.

The exposure and focus areas are separated.

The focus and exposure areas can be separated.

Hold the preview screen and the AF/AE frame will appear. Drag the frame to the desired location so that the exposure and focus areas are separated.

Panorama mode

To create a wide-angle view with panoramic mode, take several photos and stitch them together. To start the process, tap on the More option on the shooting list.

To avoid taking photos while the preview is out of the frame, make sure that you keep the image within the viewfinder.

To stop taking photos, tap on the "Stop" button. You should avoid taking pictures of backgrounds that are indistinct, such as a plain wall or an empty sky.

Food mode

lets you take vibrant images of food. Drag the frame over the highlighted area and set it to highlight.

Drag a corner to change the circular frame's size. You can also change the color tone by dragging the adjustment bar. To take a picture, tap on the desired location.

Night mode

For optimal results, use a tripod when shooting in low-light situations. It will provide you with a steadier and brighter image.

To switch to night mode, tap the More option on the shooting list.

The time indicated at the right-bottom portion of the screen will help create clearer images if you set it to Max.

Hold your device steady as the shooting session continues.

The Portrait mode ⊙ and the Portrait ⊙ video mode are both available.

With the camera, you can take photos with blurred backgrounds and the subject clearly shows itself. You can also apply effects to the background and change its appearance after you take a shot.

On the list, tap on the more option for "portrait" or "portrait video." You can then select the background effect that you want. Drag the adjustment bar to change the intensity. When Ready appears on your preview screen, tap on the video or take a picture.

Background effects

Background effect intensity
adjustment bar

The available options may change based on the shooting mode, and the settings will be applied automatically.

This feature should only be used in areas with sufficient light. However, it may not work properly in certain conditions. For instance, the device or the subject might be moving, and it might have a transparent or thin background.

Super Slow-mo mode

Slow motion captures a quick passing moment, allowing you to appreciate it later.

Tap on the More option on the shooting list and choose Super Slow-mo. You can then take a video of the moment.

To start playing Super Slow-mo video, tap the preview on the left-hand side of the screen. To start editing it, drag the section editor bar to the right or left.

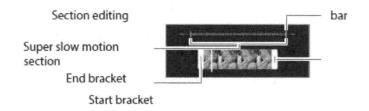

You can use this feature indoors in places with adequate light. If you shoot videos in low-light conditions, they may look grainy or dark. In some lighting conditions, like in areas with fluorescent lighting, the screen may flicker.

You can automatically record videos of super slow motion.

You can use this feature to take a quick snapshot of the moment that's about to happen in super slow motion by pressing the activate button. The preview will show the detection area for motion.

When the device detects motion, it will start recording at super slow speed and then automatically save the resulting video.

Sometimes, the recording of super slow motion might start at an unwanted moment.

The device will also record videos when objects in the detection area move toward the subject or when it shakes.

In low-light situations, such as in areas with fluorescent lights, the device can also record videos under flickering light.

Slow motion mode

You can also specify the sections of the video that will be played in slow motion for viewing enjoyment.

To start recording, tap the More option from the menu. Tap the stop button once you're done. Then, tap the preview to play the ⊚slow motion ⊙video.

To create slow motion sections, set the fast part of the video to play as a slow motion segment. Two or more will be created based on that video.

Drag the section editor bar to the right or left to change the slow motion section.

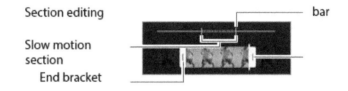

Hyperlapse mode

Capture moving subjects, such as cars or people, in hyperlapse mode and then show them as fast-moving videos. To change the frame rate, tap the More button from the menu.

If you set the device's frame rate to Auto, it will automatically adjust it based on the changing scene's speed.

Recording begins, tap to finish, and tap on the Custom settings option in the preview screen. Some features may not work with certain shooting modes.

Intelligent features

The Scene Optimizer can automatically adjust the device's color settings and apply the best possible effect to specific scenes and subjects.

The device will suggest the best composition for your picture based on its recognition of the subject's angle of interest and position.

You can set up the device to automatically scan QR codes in the preview screen if you want.

Pictures

To perform a specific action, tap the shutter button once you hold it while swiping across the screen.

The advanced options and format selection allow you to choose how to save your photos. You can take advantage of the HEIF format for high-quality images.

When using the device's built-in RAW copies feature, you can choose to save photos as uncompressed files in pro mode. These files retain all of the data in the image, but they'll take up more storage space. Each image is then saved in two different formats: JPG and DNG.

You can configure the device to automatically correct for distortion in photos taken with the ultra-wide camera.

Selfies

When there are more than two individuals in the frame, you can configure the device to take a wider-angle selfie.

Enable the device to save photos as they appear in the preview screen while you take a selfie with the front camera.

You can configure the device to set a tone for selfies. It can also use an advanced recording feature.

You can record videos with the High-Efficiency Video Codec format, which is ideal for capturing videos that are more efficient. To save the device's storage space, these files are compressed.

With the ability to create HDR10+ videos, you can enhance the contrast and color of each scene.

The device can also record sound using its zoom-in microphone. It can be used to take sound from a zoomed-in position at a higher volume.

Unfortunately, you can't play HEVC files on other devices or stream them online. Also, slow-motion videos are not supported by the device. In order to properly play the HDR10+ videos, it requires support for this format.

Shake reduction is enabled by video stabilization. It will either reduce or remove the blurry image that was caused by the camera shake while taking videos.

Useful features

Enable the device to automatically focus on a specific subject by setting it to track. When you select a subject in the preview screen, it will automatically focus on it regardless of the movement of the object or the camera's position.

The device's Auto HDR feature is useful for taking photos with vibrant colors and details in dark and bright areas.

Unfortunately, tracking a subject may fail if it's too small or too big. It can also be affected by other factors such as the subject moving too much, being in a dark place, or being backlit.

The device has a high-quality video resolution and a camera that shakes excessively. It can also zoom in and out using its optical lens and has a display viewfinder that helps you choose the right subjects.

The strength of GPS signal may decrease when it's located in areas with poor weather conditions or between buildings.

When you upload your photos to the Internet, your location may appear in them. To prevent this, deactivate the setting that allows location tracking.

You can configure the device to use different shooting modes for capturing videos and pictures.

The camera's last settings should be kept, such as shooting mode, upon launching it.

You can configure your device to vibrate automatically when the camera button is pressed and other such scenarios.

To reset the camera, go to the settings page and select "Reset." Alternatively, you can contact us by filling out the form below and we will reply to your query as soon as possible.

The app camera app and associated legal information can be viewed, though some functions may not be available on certain models.

CHAPTER FIVE

Gallery

More options Search for images.

Group similar images.

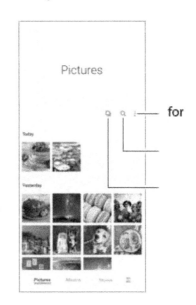

You can view and manage photos and videos that are stored on your device. You may also create albums or make stories out of them.

You can launch the Gallery app to view and manage your photos.

Grouping similar images

When you open the Gallery app you can group related pictures and set the best photos as previews for the groups. Tap the preview to see all of the pictures within each grouping.

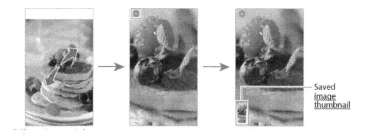

Saved image thumbnail

Viewing images

To open the Gallery app, select the image you want and swipe to the right or left to view the other files. You can also crop your photos.

To save the cropped portion of the photo, place two fingers on it. It will be saved as a file.

Viewing videos

To play videos, open the Gallery app and choose one from the list. Scroll to the right or the left to view the others.

To change the volume or brightness of the video, drag your finger across the right or left side of the screen. You can also swipe to the right or left to either fast-forward or rewind.

The videos you view are clearer and crisper than before.

You can enhance the quality of your videos by enabling the Video enhancer, which will automatically adjust the colors and brightness. You can launch the Settings app and tap on the Advanced features to activate this feature.

Although this feature is available in some apps, it can use up your device's battery. You can create albums with your photos and videos and sort them by category. You can also add items to the album and copy or move the content of your choice.

When you take or save videos and images, your device will learn your location and date, as well as the category for the photos and videos. It can also create stories and sort them by subject.

Go to the Gallery app and select the story that you want to create. You can then add or remove photos or videos by pressing the "Add or Edit" button.

Go to the Gallery app and select the "Cloud sync" option. Follow the instructions to sync the app and the cloud.

When the Gallery app is synchronized with the cloud, all of the photos and videos that you've taken will be saved there. You can view them in the Gallery app or on other devices.

When you pair your Microsoft and Samsung accounts, you can set the cloud as OneDrive.

Deleting images or videos

To remove photos or videos, go to the Gallery app and hold the image or the video you want to remove. You can then tap on the recycle bin option to get rid of the content.

Using the recycle bin feature

Keep the files that you have deleted in the recycle bin, as they will be thrown away once a certain period has passed.

To activate the recycle bin switch, go to the Gallery application and select Settings.

Go to the Gallery app and select Settings. When prompted, tap on the recycle bin switch. You can then view or download files in the recycle bin. With the Gallery app and the recycle bin enabled, you can take advantage of AR Zone's related features. You can also take advantage of its various photo and video capabilities. Launching the app is as easy as pressing the "Start" button.

Some of the features of the AR Zone app may not be available on certain models or service providers. To create an AR emoji, go to the camera app and select "Create AR Emoji." You can then take a picture of your face or tap the "Make from Pic" button to select the image.

When you tap on pre-made emojis, you can pick an expression and let it be customized. You can then follow the instructions shown on the screen to apply the emoji. Tapping on an emoji also deletes it.

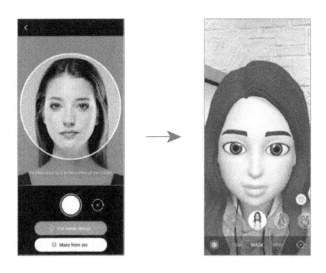

Deleting an emoji

Go to the AR Zone app and select the emoji camera. You can then manage the emojis and choose which ones you want to remove.

You can use emojis to capture fun videos or photos with the help of different shooting modes. You can launch the app and select the emoji camera.

The options for the emoji will depend on the one you've selected.

The emoji's face appears over your face, which makes it look like you're wearing a mask. It also mimics your body movements. PLAY: The emoji dances on a real-world background. You can tap the icon to take a picture or hold it to record a video.

You can customize your emoji's actions and expressions using stickers. You can use these for social networking sites or sending messages.

AR Emoji Stickers

You can make your own stickers out of your favorite emojis' actions and expressions. You can use them on social networking sites or in messages.

You can make your own stickers out of the emoji's expressions and actions. You can use them on social networking sites and in messages.

Launching the app and selecting the emoji stickers will let you make custom ones. You can then tap on the desired one and save it. You can also view the stickers that you made by tapping on the Custom option.

Deleting emoji stickers

When you open the AR Zone app, tap on the emoji stickers and choose to remove them.

You can use your emoji stickers within a chat.

You can use the emoji stickers in a message or on a social networking site. The following actions can be an example of how you can use the stickers in Messages.

To start using the AR Emoji Studio, tap on the keyboard and select the emoji icon. Then, select one of the emoji stickers that you want to use.

AR Emoji Studio

You can customize the emoji in the AR Emoji Studio and create clothes with your own patterns and colors.

After you open the ARZone app, tap on the Emoji Studio.

More options

Select an emoji to edit.

Edit the emoji.

———— Emoji icon

AR Doodle

You can create videos with drawings or virtual handwriting on the faces of pets or other individuals. When the camera is placed on a space or face, the doodle will follow that area's direction. Even if the device is moved, the doodle will remain in that space.

When the camera recognizes the subject, the area for recognition will show up on the screen. You can also draw or write in the area outside of the recognition. You can also record a video and stop it by pressing the "recording" button.

- If you tap ● and then begin to doodle, you can record yourself doodling.

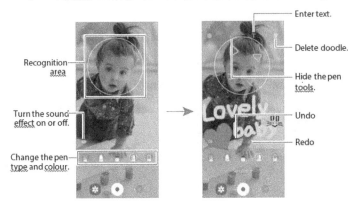

Recognition area

Turn the sound effect on or off.

Change the pen type and colour.

Enter text.

Delete doodle.

Hide the pen tools.

Undo

Redo

The Deco Pic

The Gallery app allows you to view and share videos. You can also use the Deco Pic app to take photos and record videos with the help of various stickers. The app is a part of the Bixby UI, which helps users use their device more conveniently.

CHAPTER SIX

Bixby

You can type text or talk to Bixby. It will start a function or show you the information that you want.

Although Bixby is compatible with various languages, it may not be readily accessible in certain regions.

Starting Bixby

To start using Bixby, press and hold the Side Key. The page will then appear with the Bixby intro. After you have selected the language you want to use with the app, sign in to Samsung and follow the instructions provided on the screen.

Using Bixby

Hold the Side key while pressing it and saying what you want to communicate with Bixby. Release the finger from the key and say "Hi Bixby."

For instance, while holding the Side key, you can ask Bixby to show you the current weather conditions.

Hold the Side key while pressing it and saying "Tomorrow?" to get the current conditions.

When Bixby asks you an important question while holding the side key or during a conversation, answer it or tap it.

If you're using Bluetooth audio devices or headphones and want to continue a conversation, you can do so without tapping on the icon. You can also launch the Bixby app and start a conversation using the Hands-free feature.

You can use your voice to wake up Bixby. You can start a Bixby conversation by saying "Hi, Bixby." You can then register your voice to enable the assistant to respond to your message.

Go to the Bixby app and tap on the Voice wake-up option. Then, tap the "Hi, Bixby" switch to activate it. Follow the instructions provided on the screen to complete the setup.

You can start a conversation and use text to communicate with Bixby.

Communicating by typing text

To initiate a dialogue with Bixby, open the app, tap on the desired option, and type your message. Instead of voice feedback, the assistant will respond through text.

Bixby Vision

Through Bixby Vision, users can interact with the assistant and perform various tasks by ⊙recognizing objects. This feature is useful when you need to quickly find information.

This feature might not be available or you might get the wrong results based on the size, resolution, or format of the image.

The product information presented by Bixby Vision is not the responsibility of Samsung.

Although Samsung doesn't own the product information featured by Bixby Vision, it can still launch it through one of the methods listed below. You can use the Camera app to launch it, or you can go to the Gallery app and select an image. You can also search for it using the Internet app or the app for the Internet.

When you add the Bixby app icon to the app screen, go to the Bixby Vision app and choose the feature that you want to utilize. You can also recognize text from images and documents, as well as search for similar pictures.

You can look for information about products or scan QR codes to get product details. The search results and the features that are available may vary depending on your area or provider.

Bixby Vision

You can easily add recurring routines to your device and make use of it more efficiently.

One of these is a pre-bed routine, which will help you keep your device from jarring your ears and eyes when you use it.

Adding routines

Go to the Settings app and select Advanced features and then select the "Bixby Routines" option. On the next step, you can add your own or select a routine from the list that you want to add. You can also set the conditions of the program.

To set the routine's running condition manually, tap the Start button. You can then add it to the Home screen by pressing the Add button. It will become a widget for quick access.

Recommendation list
Add your own routines.

103

Adding recommended routines

The device will start recommending features that are frequently used as routines once it learns about your usage patterns.

Tap the View all option and add the recommended routine as your own.

Tap the View all option and add the recommended routine as your own. You can also perform manual routines by pressing the Start button. Auto routines will automatically start running whenever conditions are detected.

Manual routines ▶that you set as the starting condition can be run through a button you press whenever you want.

Go to the settings app and select Advanced features. Then, go to the Bixby Routines section and select the one that you want to run. You can also tap the widget located on the home screen to complete the task.

Viewing running routines

The running routines will be displayed in the notification panel, and you can view their details by tapping on it.

You can stop running a routine by going to the notification panel and selecting "Stop."

Managing routines

Go to the Settings app and select Advanced features. Then, go to the Bixby routines section and select My routines.

To deactivate or disable a routine, tap the option that says "Deactivate" and then "Disable." You can also click on the option that says "Delete."

Multi window

The Multi window allows you to run two applications at the same time.

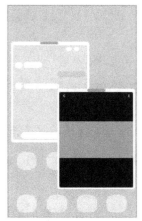

Split screen view   Pop-up view

You can also perform multiple activities simultaneously in the pop-up window.

Some apps do not support this feature. To view the list of recently used applications, tap the Recents button. Then, swipe to the right or left to open the split screen view. You can also launch another app by selecting it from the list. Launching an app from the Edge panel is done by dragging the handle to the middle of the screen.

Drag and drop an app from the left-hand screen and it will be displayed in the drop-down list. You can then choose the one that will launch in the split-screen mode.

To start an app in the split screen mode, tap the appropriate button once. You can also tap the Recents button to open the list of recently used apps and start them from the Edge panel if you want.

Adding app pairs

You can add two frequently used Edge applications to the Edge panel ➕ and start them in the split screen mode with a single tap.

To view the two apps that are currently running in the split screen, tap the circles located between the apps' windows. They will be saved as a pair in the Edge panel.

To adjust the size of the app windows, drag the circles between them up or down. The maximized window will be displayed when the circles are placed on either the top or bottom edge.

The pop-up window displays the recently used apps list. You can also swipe to the right or left and tap on an app's icon to open its screen.

When you tap the home button while using the pop-up window, it will be minimized and rendered as an app icon. You can then tap the icon again to use it.

The list of recently used apps is shown in the pop-up window, and you can launch them from the Edge panel.

Drag the handle of the Edge panel toward the center of the screen.

Drag and drop the app from the right-hand screen. It will be displayed in the pop-up window for the recently used apps list.

A new app will be launched from the list in this pop-up window after you have selected it.

Moving pop-up windows

The selected app will be launched from the pop-up window. To move the window, tap the toolbar and drag it to another location. You can also open the My Files app and manage your files.

Launch the My Files app.

To determine whether there is unnecessary data in your device's storage, tap on the Analyse storage option. Tapping on the search box will let you look for files or folders.

Clock

You can set alarms, view the current time in various cities around the world, set a specific duration, or check the time in certain events. You can also launch the Clock app.

Game Launcher

The Game Launcher is a convenient app that lets you easily access the games that you have bought from the Play Store and Galaxy Store. It also allows you to set the device to play games.

You can start the Game Launcher app and choose the game that you want.

To start the Game Launcher, go to the Settings app and select Advanced features. Then, tap the switch that will bring up the Game Launcher.

The Game Launcher will automatically show the games that you have bought from the Galaxy Store and the Play Store. If you're not able to see the games that you have bought, you can drag the Library panel up and add apps.

One of the Game Launcher's most prominent features is the ability to remove games from its list.

Drag the Library panel up and hold the game that you want to remove from the Game Launcher. You can then choose the game's performance mode.

Go to the Game Launcher app and choose the mode that you want. You can also tap on the Performance option to learn more about the app's performance.

The goal of the performance mode is to provide the best possible gaming experience.

The goal of balanced routines is to optimize the battery life and the gaming experience.

This balance ensures that the battery life is maximized while still keeping the device running smoothly. It also focuses on minimizing power consumption during gameplay.

Game Booster

Playing games with Game Booster allows participants to enjoy a better gaming experience.

When you're playing a game, go to the navigation bar and tap on the Game Booster app. Drag up from the bottom to reveal the bar if it's hidden. If you're using Swipe gestures, open the Notification Center and tap on the Game Booster icon.

You can configure the settings for Game Booster to ensure that it performs well.

In the Priority mode, you can set the device to block various notifications and incoming calls. This can help prevent the game from being disturbed.

You can also set the device to monitor temperature and memory. It will automatically adjust the video frame rate and volume to prevent the device overheating.

To hide the navigation bar's buttons, go to the navigation bar and tap on the button lock. To display the buttons, go to the navigation bar and tap on it.

The device will lock its touchscreen whenever the game is playing. To unlock it, swipe the lock icon from anywhere.

You can take screenshots with the navigation bar's buttons.

The Game Booster app can be opened from the navigation bar as long as the bar is set to swipe gestures. To activate the feature, tap on the switch that appears next to the block during the game.

The game's available options may vary. While playing, you can open apps in the pop-up windows and select the ones that you want. With the help of your smartphone, you can control your devices and manage your Internet of Things gadgets.

SmartThings app

You can learn more about this feature by launching the SmartThings app and pressing the "How to" button. You can then connect your device to the network using the instructions shown on the app. The method may vary for different types of connected gadgets and shared content.

The connectivity of your devices and the available features of their respective models may vary depending on the country.

The warranty provided by Samsung for connected devices does not cover the defects or errors that occur on them. If you notice any of these issues, you should contact the manufacturer of the device.

CHAPTER SEVEN

Sharing content

You can share content by choosing among various sharing options. For instance, you can take a screenshot using one of the options.

After you've selected an image, go to the Gallery app and choose a method that you want to share it. However, you might incur additional charges if you share files using a mobile network.

You can also share content with other SmartThings-enabled devices through Bluetooth or Wi-Fi Direct.

Go to the notification panel of the other device and swipe down. Then, tap on the 🔄 Quick Share option to activate it.

Tap 🔄 Quick Share and choose which device to send the image to. Then, accept the request to transfer.

Unfortunately, sharing videos using this feature doesn't work with SmartThings-equipped devices or televisions.

Instead, you can use the Smart View app to view content on TV.

Point your device to the other gadgets in the vicinity to share content.

Only certain Galaxy devices with the latest Ultra-Wideband technology are supported by this feature. In order to use it, the other device must have its screen turned on.

Go to the Gallery app and choose an image.

Go to the notification panel of the other device and swipe downwards. Then, tap on Quick Share to activate it.

To activate Quick Share on the other device, hold it and then tap Show my position.

Point your device at the other one and tap Quick Share. Accept the request to transfer. The feature is not supported in certain regions. You can also set who can find and send content to the other gadget.

Go to the notification panel and swipe downwards to open it. You can then tap on Quick Share to access the settings. There are three options for sharing content. You can only use this feature on Galaxy users, and everyone should be allowed to share content with their nearby gadgets.

Link Sharing

You can easily upload large files to the Samsung cloud storage server and then share them with others using a web link.

Go to the Gallery app and choose the image you want to share. You can then create a link for the image and choose a method for sharing it.

Music Share

Sharing music using Bluetooth speakers is easy with the Music Share feature. You can wirelessly play the same tracks on both your Galaxy Bud and another device.

Only certain Galaxy devices with the Music Share feature can benefit from this feature.

Only certain Galaxy devices that support Music Share can benefit from this perk. You can enjoy music on your device and another smartphone using a Bluetooth speaker.

Before you can use this feature, make sure that your Bluetooth speaker and smartphone are connected. You can also refer to the pairing guide to learn how to work with other Bluetooth devices.

Go to the notification panel of your smartphone and swipe downwards. Then, check whether Music Share is enabled.

Additional features can be used with Music Share, such as the ability to set who will share your device with.

Go to your friend's smartphone and select your Bluetooth speaker from the list.

Go to the list of Bluetooth devices and select your speaker. Now, accept the request to connect.

Your speaker will be shared.

The music that you're playing on your friend's device will be stopped once it is connected to your smartphone.

You can listen to music with your Galaxy Buds.

You can enjoy music with your friends using your Galaxy Buds. This feature is exclusive to the Galaxy Buds series, and it requires a pair of them to work. Make sure that both your smartphone and the pair of Buds are connected to each other.

Go to the notification section of your friend's phone and swipe downwards. You'll then be able to tap on Music Share to activate it.

Other features can be used by tapping and holding on the Music Share button. These include setting who will be sharing your device with.

Go to your smartphone's notification panel and swipe down. Then, tap on Media. You'll be able to select the Buds that you want to use from the list. On your smartphone, confirm the connection request and tick the boxes for your friends' devices.

To view content on a big screen, connect your device to a TV or monitor that supports screen mirroring.

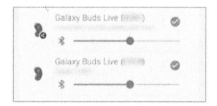

Smart View

Go to the notification panel and swipe downwards. You can then choose a device that will mirror the content of your device. The resolution of videos played using Smart View will vary depending on the model of TV.

You can access your device's data, such as messages and pictures, by connecting it to a Windows PC.

You can receive messages and calls on the computer when they come in.

This feature only works on Windows 10 1803 or higher. To fully utilize it, use the newer version of the operating system.

Connecting to a computer

To connect to a computer, go to the Settings app and select Advanced features. Follow the instructions provided on the screen to complete the process.

On the computer, open the Your Phone app and choose the category that you want to use.

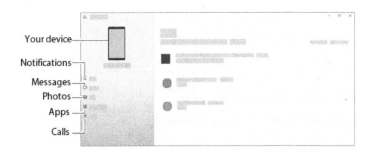

The menus and features of the device may vary based on the model or software version.

Samsung DeX

Through Samsung DeX, users can use their smartphones as a computer, a monitor, or a TV. With a keyboard and mouse, users can quickly complete their tasks on their smartphones, which are capable of displaying large screens. They can also use their devices while using Samsung DeX.

You can start using Samsung DeX and connect your device to external displays with the help of an HDMI adaptor.

Users should only use official Samsung DeX-supported accessories. These aren't covered by the company's warranty, and issues related to their usage can cause your device to malfunction.

To use the feature, you'll need to connect your smartphone to an HDMI adapter and an HDMI cable. Then, tap on the Start button on your device.

The DeX screen will appear on an external monitor or TV if you have not changed the device's screen.

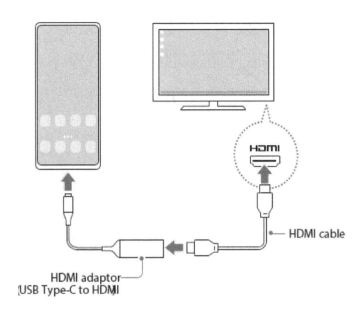

HDMI cable

HDMI adaptor
(USB Type-C to HDMI)

Wired connections to computers

Users can utilize Samsung DeX by connecting their device to a computer with a USB cable. The computer needs to have a USB-C port for this method.

To download the app for Samsung DeX, go to the company's website at www.samsung.com/dex.

To install the app, go to the website of Samsung and click on the download button. You can also connect your smartphone to the computer through a USB cable. When the device is connected, the DeX screen will show up on the computer. Users can use the feature wirelessly by connecting their smartphones to a computer or a TV.

Go to the notification panel of your smartphone and swipe downwards. You may then choose to use DeX on a computer or TV. From the list of detected devices, choose a TV or a computer. Some of these will only be detected if the mode for screen mirroring is enabled.

The computer should be connected to the same wireless network as the smartphone. The Samsung app for DeX should also be running on it.

If the connection request appears on the computer or TV, accept it. Follow the instructions provided on the screen to complete the connection and use Samsung DeX.

Make sure that the TV you plan to connect to has support for screen mirroring. You can also use a wireless mouse and keyboard to control the DeX feature. The manual for your device should provide more information.

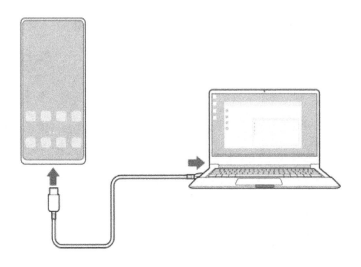

You can also set the flow of the mouse pointer from the external display of your device to the smartphone's screen. To do so, go to the Settings app and select Samsung DeX. Then, select Flow from the list of options.

The external keyboard can be used on the smartphone's screen. The device can also be used as a touchpad.

Tap on the navigation bar of your smartphone. If you enable the Swipe gesture, go to the notification panel and select the option to use your device as a touchpad.

Double-tap on the touchpad and you'll be able to see the various gestures that you can utilize with it.

The smartphone's front cover should be opened to allow you to use the device as a touchpad. If it is closed, the feature may not work properly.

Double-tapping on the screen of your smartphone will turn it on if it's not on.

You can use the keyboard on the smartphone's display. If it's not on, double-tapping on the device's screen will turn it on.

When you type text messages, make notes, or perform other actions on your smartphone's screen, a keyboard will automatically appear without needing to be connected to an external keyboard.

Controlling on a computer

You can use the keyboard and mouse to control Samsung DeX using your computer. You can easily copy and paste documents between the two devices.

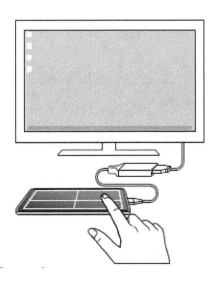

To view the various keyboard shortcuts that are available on the Samsung DeX, go to the Settings app, select General, and then click on the Physical keyboard option.

Using Samsung DeX

Your smartphone's interface is similar to that of a computer, allowing you to multitask and check the status and notifications of your device.

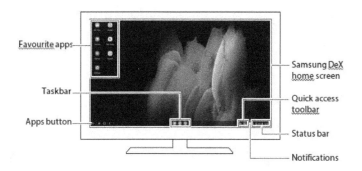

Favourite apps

Taskbar

Apps button

Samsung DeX home screen

Quick access toolbar

Status bar

Notifications

The layout of the Samsung DeX screen may vary depending on the type of device that you're using. When you start or end the feature, the apps that you're using may be closed. Some features and apps may not be available while using Samsung DeX, so you can adjust the settings by using the monitor or TV's display mode.

Go to the status bar and select Media and then select the device that you want to use for the audio output.

You can use the smartphone and Samsung DeX at the same time.

You can use the computer or an external display with separate apps for the smartphone and Samsung DeX.

While watching a video on a television or monitor, you can easily chat with one of your friends using a messenger app.

To use the app on Samsung DeX, open it on the TV or monitor and then launch another app from your smartphone.

The lock feature on Samsung DeX prevents apps from being installed and accessed while the device is being used.

You can set the lock feature for both the smartphone and the Samsung DeX screen by going to the Settings app and selecting Lock DeX.

You cannot use the Side key to lock the display of Samsung DeX and your device's screen.

You can transfer files using a computer.

Copying files

To open a file, click and hold it and choose it from the My Files app or the Gallery app on the Samsung DeX screen. Then, drag it to the computer's screen or the Gallery app.

Copying and pasting text

Copy and paste text using the keyboard shortcuts on the Samsung DeX or the computer screen. Paste it in the input field of the other device.

CHAPTER EIGHT

S Pen

The various ⊘ S Pen features are only compatible with the Galaxy S21 Ultra 5G. Users can only use these with this device. The Air command is a menu item that provides quick access to the apps that you're using regularly.

You can easily access the Air command panel by hovering your S Pen over the gadget's screen and pressing its button. Alternatively, you can also tap on the icon with the stylus.

The Air command lets you choose a specific app or function.

Pop-up windows allow you to create notes easily. You can accomplish this by double-tapping on the screen or pressing and holding the stylus button. You can also learn more about this feature through the Samsung Notes app.

You can view all of your notes in the app for Samsung Notes.

You can view all of your notes within the app or use the Smart Select feature to perform actions such as saving or sharing.

S Pen settings

You can capture screenshots to be drawn or written on them, or crop the area from which the image was taken. You can also take a quick look at the hidden content or the current content on an elongated page.

In addition, you can create and send live messages with the help of your stylus. You can either record your actions or draw a live message, which can then be saved as an animated GIF.

You can use AR Doodle to record videos with drawings or virtual notes on different surfaces, such as your face. You can also refer to this app for more information.

You can easily translate words by hovering the stylus over them. You can also post your artwork and browse the work of others.

The Bixby Vision feature can help you find related images, translate and detect text, and more.

Hovering the stylus over the screen will magnify it.

Hovering the S Pen over an app's thumbnail will open it in full screen mode.

You can use the S Pen to add vibrant colors to photos that are provided by PenUP. You can also doodle using the stylus and write or draw on a calendar app. You can add shortcuts to specific apps through the Air command.

You can use the stylus to enhance the colors in photos that are supplied by PenUP. In the Calendar app, open it, tap on the screen, and write or draw. You can also add shortcuts to specific applications through the Air button.

Air command icon

The Air command icon will stay on the screen while the panel is closed. You can open it by holding the S Pen and tapping on it.

Drag the icon to your desired location.

After you have hovered the S Pen over the screen and the Air command icon doesn't appear, you can launch the Settings app and tap on the Show floating icon to activate it.

Pen Select

When you hold the S Pen button, you can drag it across multiple items in your list or text to pick one or more of them. You can also paste or copy the selected text or items into another app and share them.

 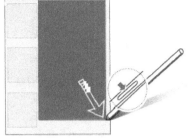

Screen off memo

You can easily create memos on the go by hovering the S Pen above the screen while it's off. You can then tap on the Save option and save the memo to Samsung Notes.

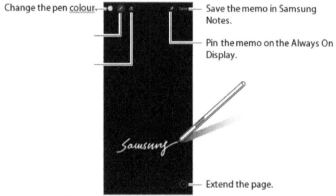

Change the pen colour.

Save the memo in Samsung Notes.

Pin the memo on the Always On Display.

Extend the page.

Change the line thickness.

If the Screen off memo feature is not activated, go to the Settings app and select Advanced features. Then tap on the Screen off memo switch.

Samsung account

You can sign in to your account and manage it through the Settings app. You can also change the settings for different connections, such as Bluetooth and Wi-Fi.

The Wi-Fi option should be activated to access the Internet or connect to other devices that use the same network.

Use Bluetooth to send or receive media files or data between other Bluetooth-enabled gadgets. You can learn more about this technology by referring to Bluetooth.

You can set your device to recognize contactless and NFC tags, which allow you to make payments using your device's built-in technology. You can also use it to buy tickets for events or make payments with the required apps.

In flight mode, you can configure your device to prevent wireless functions from working on your device. You may only use non-network services.

Follow the guidelines provided by the airlines and the instructions given by the crew members. In cases where your device is permitted to use, always use it while in flight mode.

You can configure your mobile network preferences.

You can keep track of how much data you use and customize the restrictions. You can also set your device to automatically stop using mobile data when the amount of data that you have been consuming exceeds your limit.

To prevent apps from running in the background while you're surfing the Internet, you can turn on the data saver feature.

In case you're using a Wi-Fi network connection, you can configure the apps to automatically download and use mobile data whenever there's connectivity.

You can activate your SIM cards and customize the settings for them through the SIM card manager.

Using the device as a portable hotspot allows you to share the data connection of your device with other gadgets. However, you may also end up paying extra for this feature.

Additional settings can be customized to handle different functions.

CHAPTER NINE

Wi-Fi

To use the Internet or access other devices that use the same network, activate the Wi-Fi option.

Setting up your device to connect to the Internet using a wireless network is also customizable.

To connect to the Internet, go to the Settings app and select the "Connections" option. Then, choose the network that you want to use from the list and enter the password.

The device will automatically reconnect to the Wi-Fi network once it has connected to it. It does not need a password to access the Internet every time it is available. To prevent it from connecting automatically, tap on the network and turn off the Auto reconnect feature.

Restart your device or the wireless router if you're not able to connect properly to the Internet.

The quality of the wireless network is displayed.

You can view the details of the wireless network, such as its stability and speed.

To view the Wi-Fi network quality, go to the Settings app, select "Connections," and then "Wi-Fi quality." If the quality of the network doesn't appear, go to the "Advanced" option, and then "Show network quality switch."

The quality of the connection may not be displayed for different networks.

Sharing Wi-Fi network passwords

If you want to share the password of a secure Wi-Fi network with another device, you can do so without entering it. This feature is available for both the devices that have the same contacts and the one that has the screen turned on.

Go to the Settings app and select "Connections" and then "Wi-Fi." You can also choose the network type and password from the list. After you've entered the password, your device will automatically connect to the network. You can use a feature known as Wi-Fi Direct to connect other devices to the Internet without having to set up an access point.

Go to the Settings app, select "Wi-Fi Connections" and then "Wi-Fi Direct." The detected devices will be shown.

If the device that you're trying to connect to isn't in the list, then request that it turn on its Direct feature.

Go to the Settings app and select the device you want to connect to.

When the other device accepts your Wi-Fi Direct request, your device will be connected. To end the connection, select the one that you want to disconnect from.

Bluetooth

Through Bluetooth, you can wirelessly send and receive media files or data between different Bluetooth-enabled gadgets.

It is not Samsung's responsibility to prevent the loss, misuse, or unauthorized access of data sent or received through Bluetooth.

Always ensure that the data you send and receive through Bluetooth is secure and stays with a device that is trustworthy.

Unfortunately, there are some Bluetooth-enabled devices that are not approved by the Bluetooth Special Interest Group and are not compatible with your device.

Users are urged to refrain from using Bluetooth for illegal purposes, such as illegally accessing commercial communications or pirating music files. Samsung is not liable for the repercussion of such activities.

If you're unsure if a Bluetooth-enabled device is compatible with your device, try pairing it with another Bluetooth-enabled gadget.

Pairing with other Bluetooth devices

To activate Bluetooth, go to the settings app and select "Bluetooth Connections." You'll be presented with the list of detected devices.

You can pair your device with another Bluetooth-enabled gadget by selecting it from the list.

If the device that you want to pair with isn't in the listing, then set it to Bluetooth pairing mode.

The device will be visible to other Bluetooth-enabled gadgets while the settings screen is open. You can confirm the connection request by accepting it on your device. The two linked gadgets will be connected once the other accepts the connection request. You can also unpair the two devices by pressing the "device name" button and "unpair."

Sending and receiving data

Various applications support the transfer of data using Bluetooth. You can also share media files, contacts, or other information with other Bluetooth-enabled gadgets. One example of this is sending an image to a different device.

Go to the Gallery app and select the image that you want to transfer. Then tap on the Bluetooth symbol and select the device that will receive the transferred image.

If the gadget you want to pair with doesn't appear in the list, turn on its visibility option.

Accept the request to connect with another Bluetooth-enabled device.

www.ingramcontent.com/pod-product-compliance
Lightning Source LLC
LaVergne TN
LVHW051244050326
832903LV00028B/2563